T0156819

hurricane
of thoughts

category 2

by catrina

iUniverse, Inc.
New York   Bloomington

hurricane of thoughts
category 2

iUniverse books may be ordered through booksellers or by contacting:

iUniverse
1663 Liberty Drive
Bloomington, IN 47403
www.iuniverse.com
1-800-Authors (1-800-288-4677)

Because of the dynamic nature of the Internet, any Web addresses or links contained in this book may have changed since publication and may no longer be valid. The views expressed in this work are solely those of the author and do not necessarily reflect the views of the publisher, and the publisher hereby disclaims any responsibility for them.

ISBN: 978-1-4502-6538-6 (sc)
ISBN: 978-1-4502-6539-3 (ebk)

Printed in the United States of America

iUniverse rev. date: 10/13/2010

that day in may

magical whispers that start the morning
every single thing about you i am adoring
intertwined in the softness of your embrace
here i will stay with you in our special place

sharing a love that is so beautiful and true
beating heart is so lost in wonderful you
my soul is wrapped up in your tenderness
butterflies take me higher with each kiss

happiness overcame life's tortured pain
falling in love with you over and over again
amazing touch that takes my breath away
rest of our life was born that day in may

innocent lives

mean and evil; a society of hate crimes
your decision to extinguish innocent lives
we are not all the same
always judging people you cannot change

thinking you are better because someone is black
prejudice society; this certainly is not a fact

just because a man or woman is gay
beating them is not going to change their ways

religious beliefs that are different than yours
does not give you the right to scorn

when the smoke clears; where will you be
you die; and your soul will never be free

mean and evil; a society of hate crimes
your decision to extinguish innocent lives
we are not all the same
always judging people you cannot change

two hearts that cared

thought we were building our paradise
now your gone; it leaves me so sick inside
seeing you out takes my breath away
i smile; so you think everything is okay

into this full length mirror i stare
it is your emotional scar i wear
falling asleep; you are in my dreams
everyday, wishing you were here with me

such a hard game to play
this horrible heartache
missing you; hurt, my heart cannot bare
our song plays; two hearts that cared

goodbye is so hard to say

shortened beginning
pain you are supplying
so tired of trying
thoughts are crying
broken heart is dying

how can you do this to me
why can't we be
i want you to want me

our love wasn't true
romance has no more room
can't live without you
what else can i do
one foot in the tomb

how can you do this to me
why can't we be
i want you to want me

needing you for keeps
empty well; dark and deep
where jaded tears weep
creeping thru cracks of concrete
worn shutters finally sleep

a second chance

seems dreams are falling into suspicion
a need to disappear like a magician

a repetitive cycle that needs to break
no longer living in your life of deception and hate

living in shadows; a hunger no longer
stepping out to be a leader not a follower

look inside; seek what you need to find
befriend only those people of like mind

soul searching for a serenity of silence
desperate need of change; a second chance

away from home

loving hearts that cared
once a beautiful love all shared
within my arms; you i would hold
a forever promise to never let you go

then it came like once in a blue moon
you left me cold and empty in this room
tick, tock; the hands on the clock
are we stuck or did it just stop

survival of love should stand on it's own
what is it that drives us away from home
so many hearts continue to break
how much more can we take

our beautiful children; for god sakes
when will we stop teaching our own hate
our great poisonous escape
it is our world that we shape

silence enters the room

silence enters; like lightning across the sky
blank stare; i can taste the poison in your eyes
evil that lurks with the smirk on your face
leaving me alone in this dark place

remembering that broken promise with a smile
my empty, beating heart; lost in a land of exile
forced to live, learn and create a life of change
picking up pieces; just mirrored images of pain

inhibited emotions of love; heavy dismay
shame; the lies, deceit and your manipulating way
karma has her say; even in early of your end
splattered tears; wondering, when did this begin

tomb of concrete

you visit my tomb of concrete
there you stand; week after week
a bouquet of flowers you leave
watered; with your lies and deceit

your actions my heart could not condone
you sit in your misery of all alone
praying for forgiveness; wishing i was home
cold rush of my blood, enters your bones

you cry and try to apologize
tears race from your bloodshot eyes
a broken soul, gone and on the rise
i can still hear your deep sighs

no longer living with what you did to me
my lifeless shadow haunts your every dream
you beg for peace; in search of harmony
a promise i will keep; never letting you be

a bouquet of flowers you leave
watered; with your lies and deceit
there you stand; week after week
you visit my tomb of concrete

my heart skips

our romance; the teasing, the play
never imagined falling in love this way
even in silence we have a wonderful time
you know i am yours and i know you are mine

another dimension your beautiful smile takes me
an amazing love affair; together, we will always be
your eyes as blue as the deepest of seas
every time i look at you i sink into ecstasy

your soft touch that cradles my soul
it is to the end of time with you i want to go
mesmerized and tantalized by your kiss
the way you make me feel; my heart skips

your own skin

do not feed the hate; this is where we all need to begin

why drown your precious soul in a world of sin

let go of the past hurt and pain; start learning to forgive

save yourself; for this only comes from deep within

riches of life; love one another, it is the only plan

magnificent peace surrounded by beautiful family and friends

simply love the gorgeous life you have been given to live

changes you can make are found under your own skin

another dark day

full moon hangs over another dark day
it seems nothing ever goes my way
the stairs i try to climb are so long
trying to find my weary soul back home

tears travel the cracks of the hardwood floor
give me strength; please, i need so much more
the same old song and dance
reflection of change the only chance

over the scattered pieces of my heart
i must crawl to reach my new start
it seems nothing ever goes my way
full moon hangs over another dark day

puddles of pain

here alone i sit in a melancholy hell
trying to break free from your unwanted spell
feeling of loneliness consumes my mind
all the lies you told were so unkind

the days filled with so much sadness
trying to survive these hours of madness
living within my walls of silence
clipped wings leaving me flightless

every night i cry my weary eyes to sleep
waking constantly to your evil in my dreams
hurting inside; my heart is broken
our lost love; my breaths are choking

words just cannot explain how i feel
time is all i need for this heart to heal
it is raining all over again
tears forming puddles of pain

silent wings

my entire life; where have you been
your anticipated touch lives under my skin
happiness we share is so very special to me
together; you and i will make memories

your beautiful soul is all my eyes see
each kiss; sharing the air we breathe
holding hands; just us, forever and a day
into my future it is you i am going to take

on cloud nine above our love floats
forever promise to never give up hope
sharing a love like a fairy tale; but true
on silent wings; into my life you flew

death row inmate

in a one room prison cell; lonely, there you sit
cold blooded murder; a crime you did commit
three meals a day and sheltered from the storm
they keep you behind walls away from societies harm

country we live in protecting the convict not the victim
something seriously wrong with our judicial system
you cry and claim the form of execution is inhumane
even poor, unwanted animals are treated the same

year after year; defense attorney; appeal after appeal
governor grants your stay after yet another last meal
a new day; huddled in a corner praying for your fate
good verses evil; you are merely a death row inmate

shallow graves

our government; just dictates

shallow graves
a society digs
sex, pain and hate
a society creates

lies, manipulation and deception
government takes possession
no privacy, big brother
government; we need another

democracy; they say
government fueling hate
country of greed
government takes the lead

shallow graves
a society digs
sex, pain and hate
a society creates

our government; just dictates

last dance

the blood is draining from my heart
from my swollen eyes pails of tears part
memories of us my mind tries to erase
after all you've done; why do i miss your embrace

it was only you that threw our love away
my broken heart trying to survive another day
what we shared; was it the wrong kind of right
floating off into nightmares night after night

emotional pain; twisted and tangled in sheets
your evil ways taking my soul away for keeps
this life of mine meant to be lived alone
at least until you bring your love back home

the candle we lit has lost its light
never looking back you walked out of sight
all i wanted was our love to have a chance
all you wanted was my very last dance

slice of heaven

anticipation; touch and caress of your soft skin
back to that place where our love did begin
it is your beauty my imagination can see
holding you tight; dancing with you in my dreams

possession of lovely charisma and charm
always protecting my feelings from harm
captivated by your sparkling blue eyes
heart flies away on the winds to the sky

the scent of you constantly surrounds me
escape of our soul; two bodies set free
my fingertips trace the lines of your lips
into a daydream i drift; to meet your kiss

amazing smile that just blows me away
there is only one more thing to say
appreciation; gorgeous life i have been given
this world; you are my beautiful slice of heaven

tears I cry

your thoughtless, uncaring way
left my soul in such dismay
loneliness fills the air in this room
you said you promised the moon

playing with distraught emotions
just another one of your tokens
no apologies; you show no shame
was our relationship merely a game

you left my life so shattered and empty
someone else looked more tempting
remembering your heartless lie
bathing in the falling tears i cry

house of hell

your negative ways consume my aching mind
controlling actions; manipulating and unkind
so many emotional games you play
living like a scavenger; day after day

a bitter creature lurking in the night
the way you hurt is not at all right
evil inside, you are a devil in disguise
preying on true love and angel eyes

all the fancy things your soul craves
not knowing love; it is the way you behave
shattered heart; no hope for repair
another lie; acting as if you cared

destroyed by your sharpened claws
pictures of us that lined our walls
happiness our beautiful home once held
short moment of time became a house of hell

blackened tears leaving tracks on my cheeks
gone; taking everything, my soul is weak
parading around like you are a casanova
searching for another victim; another lover

you i adore

just like the sun that shines in the sky
you brighten every single day of my life
like a fragrant flower that blooms after a spring rain
deep within my soul; feelings i have for you remain

like the shiny moon that glows in the dark night
you light up my life; my heart takes flight
you are as beautiful as picture perfect art
with your hands you hold each beat of my heart

as the leaves play and dance in the trees
you are the soft breeze beneath my wings
the birds chirping the melodies they sing
every night i carry your sweet voice in my dreams

just like the prettiest of two white doves
marvelous emotion we share; our amazing love
you are everything i want and even more
in my heart forever; it is only you i adore

one more day

holding your picture in my hand so tight
wishing you were here with me tonight
living in this life of my misery
here alone is not where i want to be

drowning in the sorrows of my tears
missing your touch for all these years
every single night unable to sleep
mind engulfed in constant sad dreams

a broken soul unable to move on
lost in the words of our romantic song
in this cold, empty room i lay
dying a little more every single day

the scent of your skin is all i know
so very young, why did you have to go
the heavens took you away from me
clouds above; i pray, give me strength

i can see you walking toward me
so real it seems but only a dream
i would give my last breath away
to have you in my arms one more day

end of your world

slowly the pendulum swings; seconds tick away
lingering in pity; you waste another priceless day
your self imposed chains have enslaved your soul
sinking deeper into the unknown; no other place to go

confidence turns to tragedy; your end is very near
creeping so close; the cry, destruction overpowers fear
a broken and battered heart is tired of paying the price
pills for the numbing; razor blade tempts your sacrifice

a happy life that no longer exists on the horizon
death and the prince of darkness are now your liaison
lying in a sea of flames that lines hell's corridor
you sought your light at the end of your world

old porch swing

here i sit alone on our old porch swing
i am missing you; my wonderful everything
witness to another beautiful, yellow sunrise
i want to gaze into your amazing blue eyes

birds sitting in the trees singing a melody
i daydream and wish you were here with me
enjoying the mist of a quiet, falling rain
come home; my beating heart is feeling pain

white, puffy clouds that dance across the sky
my thoughts consumed by only you and i
colorful flowers bloom to enjoy a beautiful day
wanting your softest touch that takes me away

butterflies glide and play in a spring breeze
the love i have for you is all i want and need
darkness falls; the orange sun gaining ground
my imagination feels you all around

moon soars to the top of the sky on a starry night
it is only you in my dreams; our love takes flight
i am missing you; my wonderful everything
here i sit alone on our old porch swing

wonderful you

it is your love that makes my heart beat
and a soft touch that makes my knees weak
i look into your eyes; it is a beautiful flower i see
and your amazing love i feel inside of me

passion we crave for one another; you are mine
this love we share only comes once in a lifetime
my fantasies and dreams have come true
all along it has been wonderful you

my history

you are hateful, mean, cruel and rude
wondering; minute to minute what you will do
holding on to someone who will not be real
everlasting, true love my soul wants to feel

voice of sanity lingers inside of me
wide open eyes; now i can honestly see
without you; i thought i would just die
realizing all you do is try to make me cry

childish games you continue to play
denying each one of them in your own way
your senseless lies are getting old
time for me to leave you out in the cold

tomorrow is another beautiful day
without you; i am well on my way
lovers or friends we will never be
you are a fixture of only my history

pages of my diary

it is the simple smile you put on my face
no one in this world can ever take your place
empty pieces of paper to fill
writing of a true love that is so real

amazing feeling my pen pours on the pages
you are the greatest treasure i have felt in ages
we dance with each word i write
wishing you were here so i can hold you tight

you come alive when i reread the lines
falling in love with you time after time
with all these wonderful memories i am blessed
you certainly live within this heart in my chest

our amazing love affair will always remain
it lives on these pages in between
you would understand what you mean to me
if you could read the pages of my diary

best friends

you have always been there when i call
wiping my tears even before they fall
no matter the time; you run to hold me tight
even when my swollen eyes can't sleep at night

you open my mind to happiness i need to seek
just when my heart is breaking and feeling weak
picking me up after i've fallen off my toes
you help me focus on my future goals

in your calm voice you remind me of what matters
even if the pieces of my heart are so scattered
everything we do for each other will never change
because we will always be best friends

just one dream

another lonely, dark, saturday night
full moon rests in the star filled sky
here i lay in the shadows of my pain
putting pieces of my heart together again

glassy, swollen eyes; where my tears weep
puddles soak the white, bedroom sheets
memories of us engulf my weary mind
those beautiful days where love was kind

life seems so incomplete without you here
you don't miss me; that is so very clear
wanting, needing you to love and hold me
if i had one dream tonight; just one dream

you are

you are the yellow sun in my rise
you are the softness of a cloud in the sky
you are the glow in my moonlight
you are the sparkling star in my eye

you are the beauty in my dreams
you are the warmth in my sleep
you are the light in my fire
you are the one and only i desire

you are the deepness of my sea
you are the one who completes me
you are the wind beneath my wings
you are nothing less than my everything

shallows of misery

day after day i sit waiting; my mind lost in wonder
all i hear is the rolling distant cries of thunder
holding on tightly to my fairy tale dreams
waiting for a special someone; forever it seems

shadows dance in the moonlight with a flickering candle
spending my life alone is more than i can even handle
time ticks on by and my soul ages another day
for it is only you i need; please, take me away

from my bleeding, broken heart so much pain seeps
even when i sleep; from swollen eyes, tears weep
often daydreaming of a true love just for me
as i lie here in the darkest, shallows of misery

another day

i want to wake; another day
with the same smile on my face
the beautiful sunrise
that pierces my eyes

birds chirping in the wind
happy to be here again
butterflies that dance in the sky
another beautiful day in july

moon glows, fireflies fly
floating on clouds in the sky
storms of shooting stars
make a wish to no more scars

forgiveness and faith
let's go to the next day
with the same smile on my face
i want to wake; another day

old dirt road

here i stand; on our old dirt road
where my soul now walks alone
lined along our pond; where we would swim
the cattails sway and dance in the wind

worn path; where we would go horseback riding
i wish you had told me those feelings you were hiding
our names carved in the overgrown oak tree
with love; here, where you promised me

our fire pit; where we held hands in the rain
the flame has died; my heart is in pain
wide open field; where we stared at the moon
you will never know how much i adored you

still missing the years you were mine
trying to survive one day at a time
where my soul now walks alone
here i stand; on our old dirt road

february

your mesmerizing eyes taking me away
i will never forget that amazing day; in february
this life of mine will never be the same
your kindness rescued my heart from pain

you and i are like birds of a feather
enjoying every moment we spend together
every day we make a new memory
all we need to be complete is just you and me

your touch that vibrates thru my soul
a life of happiness is our only goal
a marvelous love your feelings display
everyday i wake it is you i crave

my love is so lost in the beauty of you
sharing a wonderful life of forever true
your mesmerizing eyes taking me away
i will never forget that amazing day; in february

coffin of nails

here i stand before you; my precious lord
was it the incredible life you gave i did not adore
family and friends gather; tears they weep
inside these pine walls my body forever sleeps

pain and agony drench the path i have chosen
here i lie; my soul left empty and frozen
senses failed; i did not see all that was there
looking for love in shadows that were unclear

my destination and fate in the midst of receiving
all that was needed; just a love of believing
for one more chance; it is your seas i would sail
instead i lie suffocating in this coffin of nails

happiness

years pass us by living in sorrow
one relationship after another; smiles we borrow
happiness is the key to success
it lives in your heart; no need to second guess

happiness is something we all seek
you have to open your eyes instead of peek
key to happiness is you; this is very true
an emotion that lives right inside of you

happiness is found in family and friends
this is certainly where it all begins
live your life doing things right; don't live in a mess
you must love yourself to conquer happiness

linger in your midst

my soul is stuck on our songs
wondering; where i went wrong
it's so hard; i don't understand
how you could just let go of my hand

i can't sleep; i can't breathe
all i want; is you here with me
why do i think about you all the time
it is as if you are still mine

my heart needs hemmed and boxed in
sometimes i feel like i'm suffocating
some days i can barely drag out of bed
hours pass by; wishing, i was dead

things can't always be the same
simply; needing to forget your name
all these thoughts of you i need to resist
forever; is too long to linger in your midst

my happy ending

first moment i saw you i thought i would die
sincerity in your eyes made me melt inside
everything you say and do is so pleasing
your beautiful smile makes my life so easy

i feel your amazing soul with me everyday
your gentle touch takes my breath away
you are everything i want and need
the love of my life you are indeed

all of my future dreams have come true
here i sit; all of my heart so lost in you
it was your love from the very beginning
i will never let you go; my happy ending

narcissistic mood

you parade around like you do nothing wrong
every time you speak out loud you lack charm
always looking in the mirror; you are so vain
you only strive to cause innocent people pain

always running off with that big mouth
when things don't go your way; you pout
poking fun at the less fortunate; you are so cruel
imaginary friend; the only one you had in school

putting down people and all the good they do
deep inside you wish their success belonged to you
always playing games trying to get someone's goat
in the end; you really are the butt of the jokes

thinking you are important with all of this disorder
but in reality; to society, you are just plain horror
so damn sick of your me, me, me attitude
here you go again with your narcissistic mood

promise of change

thru the deep, dark forest i will run
to the stream; sorrows i will drown
thoughts of you cross my mind
how is so much love so unkind

breeze thru the trees; talk to me
beautiful flowers in bloom; i cannot see
sun in the sky; rays, a hope for life
daily struggles putting up a fight

here where my dreams come alive and play
overgrown field; where my broken body lay
my cheeks; home to the tears that weep
you stole my beating heart; for keeps

over and over i recite your name
to my soul; a promise of change
thru the deep, dark forest i will run
to the stream; sorrows i will drown

day after day

convinced this life was meant to be spent alone
day we met, you touched my soul and took me home

different from the others; you are one of a kind
you; the truest of love, i finally did find

wonderful love affair only two people can share
feeling inside, how much you really do care

thoughts of you consume my busy mind
deep down within my soul i know you are mine

your beautiful voice serenades my kiss
i cherish every moment of this wonderful bliss

every night; within my dreams you drift
our life spent together; such an amazing gift

you and your wonderful love swept my heart away
with you is where i want to stay; day after day

portrait of us

taking a drive in the country on a cloudy day
years it's been since i've visit our hideaway
cob webs fill the broken panes of glass
entire place surrounded by overgrown grass

fishing poles and tackle weathered and worn
so many memories we shared; my heart is torn
the flowers are dead that lined our porch
still sitting by the door; our fire pit torch

many bird nests rest in the rafters above
i've missed sharing this place with you my love
musty smell of a fresh, fallen rain fills the air
where you would nap; there sits your chair

wood is stacked; many cold winters never touched
rug where we would snuggle; you made me blush
all that is left on the mantle; covered in dust
our wedding day; my favorite portrait of us

my own tranquility

the power you have controls my every move
i haven't the strength to leave our bedroom
staring at our blank walls; lost in a haze
feeling like i haven't slept for decades

all of my thoughts of you are lifeless
alone; you ripped my heart out of my chest
drowning my soul in puddles of tears
letting you win; i have wept for years

you were my dreams; now i am so very lost
swimming in love notes and pictures tossed in a box
hoping my closed eyes will finally see
climbing the walls of my own tranquility

bridges

they said i did this and i did that
thinking; i just wear many hats
thought i had them from the beginning
now it looks like my own ending

into the mirror i just stare
i see a frown and blond, spiked hair
drowning in my many told lies
friends; they saw it in my eyes

here i sit between my four walls
never; not one friend ever calls
this air i breathe is ever so frigid
i have burned; every one of my bridges

you love me

peaceful sounds of another beautiful morning
it is your wonderful love i am so adoring
magnificent pink and orange sunrise
we sit and gaze into each others eyes

birds harmonize the poetic melodies
the way you love me puts my soul at ease
dew drips from the leaves of the trees
enjoying every moment you spend with me

white, puffy clouds dance across the blue sky
start of an amazing day; just you and i
bumble bees buzz and take flight
daydream of yet another magical night

hummingbirds flutter around the hibiscus flower
it is your unselfish, caring way my heart devours
mother nature's display of marvelous beauty
i thank the heavens above that you love me

my precious pain

your amazing kiss set my lonely soul on fire
from the bottom of my heart; you were my desire
your love; you convinced me to never, ever fear
daily; drowning in a puddle of my many tears

talk of marriage and raising our own family
thoughts in a whirlwind; how could you leave me
my bleeding heart has been torn in two
part of me is lost in so much love for you

your broken promise to always love only me
i'm left living alone in your lies and deceit
the hurt i feel is driving me completely insane
trying to erase you from my world; my precious pain

amazing cool breeze

gray clouds lie beneath the heavens above
birds; we can hear the different sounds of love
thunder echoes thru the valley of the trees
creating a natural melody; raindrops tap the leaves

lightning strikes and lights up the dark, summer sky
wildlife scurries thru the woods back home to hide
under the stars we sleep on a moonlit night
as close as we can get, holding each other tight

morning arrives along with a fresh new day
just you and i; whatever we do, come what may
smell of brewed coffee fills the country air
vacation from the city; not one single care

the water on the lake as smooth as can be
sun peeks out to shine down on you and me
beautiful day of peace and quiet; our souls at ease
in the air we breathe lives an amazing cool breeze

it is you

it is you; that puts a smile on my face

it is you; that brightens my everyday

it is you; that makes my heart race

it is you; that takes my breath away

it is you; that i want to embrace

it is you; that touches my soul with beauty

it is you; the sweet smell i taste

it is you; that wipes my tears on a gray day

it is you; that takes me to a magical place

it is you; i will always call my baby

my beautiful love

overgrown path lined with mossy rocks and fallen dreams
last time i saw you; it has been eternity it seems
walking thru the woods as darkness falls
i hear your voice; my name, for which you call

noises that creep in the silence of the night
going to check on you to be sure you are alright
my promise; i was your lover and always your friend
the thoughtlessness and evil, committed sin

rush of a damp cold enters every one of my bones
marker i placed to tell me i'm upon your home
footprints in front of me remind me of where i've been
old oak tree where your noose hung from that limb

sorrow takes over; my tears water the flowers i placed
beauty is dead; my love for you will never be replaced
time to go live with the angels in the stars above
here to say goodbye one last time; my beautiful love

coldest day in july

you talk and can't even look me in the eye
telling one lie after another lie
your heart is made of nothing but stone
wish you had just left my love alone

my words were nothing less than true
how am i going to survive my life without you
i do; was a fake promise that left your lips
sealed with a so called forever, loving kiss

all of our goals and many future dreams
washed away in a rainy, summer breeze
your actions are so evil and cruel
i wish my fragile soul had never met you

icicles roll off my cheeks; so many tears
my entire life; this is my worst year
walking away; leaving me high and dry
today has to be the coldest day in july

in this hammock with you

lightning strikes and an occasional thunderstorm
rain pours; feeding all the new life we so adore
we have waited so long; here it is summertime
our favorite season where most days the sun shines

birds perched on the branches of so many trees
we wake to the sunrise and their amazing melodies
flowers bloom to the birth of the new sunlight
sharing these moments with you just feels so right

taking in the wonderful smell of fresh cut grass
all those cold, damp days are gone at last
breeze blows and the leaves do their dance
our most beautiful start to a new romance

colorful butterflies paint such a pretty day
taking in every single moment come what may
bees buzz thru the air collecting pollen and nectar
i don't care what we do as long as we are together

the bright full moon shines in the dark night
we wish upon a shooting star that glides across the sky
taking in the beauty of yet another day in june
here i want to stay; in this hammock with you

last letter written

it was your touch; your love and affection
i fell hard and lost my very own direction
i wanted to spend the rest of my life with you
fantasy i felt in my heart turned out to be untrue

i often wonder why things are not the same
my broken heart carries so much sorrow and pain
such a lack of you has left me all alone
how can i survive all these memories of our home

i can still hear your voice in every single room
my love for you stretches far past the moon
my reflection in the mirror shows nothing but tears
thoughts of you has taken my life of many years

words i cannot say just pours out onto paper
our relationship disappeared like some sort of vapor
for you my love; i am still so very smitten
wish i could send you my last letter written

same sob story

like a rock on water; you skip thru life
help you seek is always someone's sacrifice
your stories are manipulating and never jive
thinking friends are stupid; they have open eyes

always running around; soul stuck on empty
wishing others would open their heart and see
lies you tell; you have convinced yourself well
everyone is against you; who created this hell

telling others that your friends are mean
they know you live in the same dull routine
the life you live in all your sick vanity
your deceit drives everyone to insanity

lack of strength; year after year living off scars
cherished friendships are emotionally charred
your righteous soul and all of your glory
it is the victim you portray; same sob story

chapters

everyday; is a lesson to be learned
at times we live without concern
the pages of our lives turn

acceptance and popularity; just a few things
every boy or girl; wants to be king or queen
in this life; there is so much more to see

we walk thru daily stages
sometimes; we feel like we live in cages
time to turn to the next pages

so many lose sight and want to fight
bad day; claim, they have no rights
open your eyes and look high into the sky

when you reach your end
did your soul live in sin
chapters; do you need to read again

hear you breathe

please don't walk away from me
it is your love that my soul needs
i want to build my life around you
i know you can feel it; what i say is true

for you; i would swim the roughest sea
it is only your words i truly believe
i am grateful for your amazing love
with you; i can touch the stars above

i want to hold you tight every single night
what we share just feels so very right
for you; i would walk thru a roaring fire
you are in my heart; you are my desire

that beautiful soul of yours; i so adore
you are the one i have been waiting for
i'm begging; please don't leave me
always wanting to hear you breathe

under a shade tree

in a summer breeze; under a shade tree
you pulled me closer; then, you kissed me
my knees buckled and butterflies raced
you put an everlasting smile on my face

my heart pounds like a beating drum
i never thought i would fall in love
you are the most beautiful soul in my life
sent from the heavens above; so divine

the sparkle in your eyes takes me away
i will never forget that amazing day
you pulled me closer; then, you kissed me
in a summer breeze; under a shade tree

harden my heart

there was a day when you took me higher
all your silent lies; i have lost my desire
i gave you every single ounce of my energy
alone; you destroyed you and me; completely

go live that life you claim feels so right
i do not want someone like you in my life
you think the grass is greener on the other side
there will be a day when your tears cry

you tried to run my heart thru the mud
telling people things i have never done
figured out the type of person you are
i made it thru all your emotional scars

i stare into the mirrors of my mind
my message to you; this is the last goodbye
you do not know and certainly the worst part
your cruel words managed to harden my heart

if walls could talk

tons of calls to our emergency 911
no one will come until something goes wrong
every swing is for you; the batterer
no one will help; does it really matter

without you i cannot breathe
then your fist; again, hits me
who is that; a distraught soul
stuck in your world; no place to go

each bruise has it's very own story
fading colors; your moment of glory
is it cry wolf; until someone is dead
my soul called so many months ahead

when your fist hits me
with you; i will no longer breathe
if i don't leave, this will never stop
my only wish; if walls could talk

wishing well

smile you display when i see you out
you have no idea how my heart pounds
you enter the room and glide across the floor
it is you; my wanting eyes so adore

that wonderful charisma you display
i crave you in every single, little way
i am fascinated with your amazing mind
you are that someone that is my kind

your heart beats ever so tenderly
every night; i think of you with me
my secret; that i will never tell
last penny dances into the wishing well

pillow talk

lying next to you; another beautiful sunrise
rays of light stretch thru the window blinds
with you; all the love in my heart lies
i wake and i'm instantly lost in your eyes

we share our very first morning kiss
each moment i spend with you is full of bliss
we discuss our days spent as little kids
laughing at all the silly things each of us did

all the times we thought it was in love we fell
even deep conversation of what truly was hell
vacations and the most amazing attractions we've seen
we chat about our personal secrets and our dreams

exchanging our desires and our future goals
it is only you i want to see when i come home
hours pass us by; tick tock, the bedside clock
i so love our time spent during pillow talk

too late to apologize

you knew i would always be there
took advantage of how much i cared
falling for your lies about true love
you are not what dreams are made of

with your lips; i use to share a kiss
infidelity; ruined our moments of bliss
sun sets and the distant moon rises
you live a life of many disguises

had a meeting with my sad soul
letting your cruel and evil ways go
everyday gets brighter and brighter
finding myself; i get higher and higher

since you have been gone; i am happy
music to my ears; such a beautiful melody
not going to believe anymore lies
for you; it is, too late to apologize

from the beginning

loving you is a crime in some countries
punishable by law; we can't be you and me
science and religion says it's a choice
you need to really listen to our voice

the bible condemns us to earth's hell
already there; i can handle afterlife well
society thinks their opinion is always correct
we are a people; victim of so much prejudice

slavery; just a pure cruel world in which we live
people all around us living in a life of sin
poisoned by music, movies, games and our tv
when will every one open their eyes and see

our government; on the edge of communism
we just sit and wait for the next changing season
two political parties split; no one can agree
our humanity might become a piece of history

quiet mouths really show we are weak
no one to blame but those who do not speak
we are here to love one another unconditionally
that was the rule above; from the beginning

never on the wall

i don't have time for heartache and pain
just wanting someone that will remain
so scared to give anyone another chance
until that night; we shared a beautiful dance

with you, my open emotions fly so very high
convinced; fairy tales are no longer a lie
listening to your promises; no doubt in my mind
tearing each of my walls down; one at a time

reflection of you and your love in my eye
my soul sparkles like a bright star in the sky
day came and you brought that tear to my eye
can't give me all of you; you never told her goodbye

struggles with relationships that never last
always meeting the one lost in their past
loved those big hearts you use to draw
the real writing was never on the wall

shades of blue

the damp, shallow grave calls to you by name
the choices you make; life will never be the same
soul is tangled and lost in the house of sin
candlelight flickers with the cold, blowing wind

bloodshot eyes on the stars above; needing proof
stumbling on a spiral staircase in search of truth
death song sings from the strings of a violin
every note strikes a cord deep down within

perched on hell's gate; vultures sit and just wait
every single ounce of your soul they will desecrate
patiently satan takes; adding many to his long list
with your fate you fight; clinched are tight fists

harmonious harp plays her beautiful, loving melody
follow the angels to eternal life; forever divine will be
darkness looms; covering the sky in an amazing hue
full moon dances with the different shades of blue

old jewelry box

wonderful day at the park playing with the kids
there lies the 4 leaf clover we found by the jungle gym
the seasoned newspaper clipping; grandma's obituary
i so miss sharing with her; the days of my history

wallet size picture of us; me and my siblings
rare time spent together; everyone with a family
broken petals from that beautiful pressed flower
loss of a best friend; i will never forget that hour

birthday card from mom and dad; signed we love you
my beating heart; so grateful for all that they do
the cross i received that day i went to church
so many memories in my head and some hurt

lifting the lid; wondering what i would find
gasping for air; holding back tears i want to cry
ring you bought me lies next to my first watch
has been years since i opened that old jewelry box

dirty, little secret

she's slipping away; you always defend her actions
over stepping my authority; offering her satisfaction
with friends for the weekend; i found her diary
and what i read has come as such a shock to me

she was just a little girl playing in her room
you promised her everything; even the moon
you stripped an important part of her life away
repeating your sick acts; day after day

you would enter her bed as she slept at night
touching inappropriately; knowing it was not right
our daughter; so withdrawn, so very pretty
emotional scars you've caused without any pity

you are a monster without a care in the world
how could you hurt our innocent, little girl
will not let you get away with this and live in regret
i know everything; even your dirty, little secret

lost in thought

trying to hold my head high with a smile
knowing it is only going to last a little while
missing you with every ounce of my being
day to day; praying for even more healing

sometimes i can't even feel my heart beat
at night when i sleep; nightmares creep
cold tears run down both of my sad cheeks
lost in a world without you; been here for weeks

so many empty evenings spent here all alone
this worn out soul no longer has a happy home
you were the only one; it was love i sought
now i just sit here in the dark; lost in thought

the cemetery trees

full moon guides my soul in your direction

here to help you; offering you some satisfaction

doe carved in stone; under a pile of dirt he sleeps

moon rises and darkness falls; his ground, he creeps

another world needs all the good that you do

open your heart and feel it to be true

a lost soul reliving his very darkest, last hours

just waiting for the sun to rise and dust to devour

light is bright on the path ahead of me

i can hear your cries thru the cemetery trees

complete stranger

i stare at my broken, mirrored emotions
you left without even a single word spoken
like a lifeless leaf stripped from a tree
you left my future incomplete and empty

imperfections i see in my own eyes
caused by all of your hurtful, heartless lies
just a simple thought of the cruel you
in a flash; you can change my mood

these tears i cry flood my shallow heart
all of my memories of you; they must part
once, there was a beginning; now, only an end
in time i will move on and start all over again

now; you need me and want me to care
you lost your chance; i was already there
your words empower me without any anger
walking away from you; complete stranger

unwanted tears

saying you love me; what was i going to gain
living in your past not dealing with the pain

why; on my knees praying above
my feelings you took advantage of

all my love was genuinely true
walking away like i was a hobby to you

bleeding heart smeared all over the pavement
did not know you lived with so much hatred

all my precious time i wasted
so many unwanted tears i have tasted

love, loving you

every moment we spend together feels so right
you are the most beautiful change in my life
not a thing in this world will ever compare
to the pitter-patter feeling i have for you my dear

it is your marvelous self i crave
wanting to feel you in my arms everyday
by the shadows of the flickering candle light
together we slowly dance into the night

your soft kiss feeds my wanting desire
touching your body takes me even higher
stuck in my heart; forever and true
into you i have fallen; i so love, loving you

i even cried

knowing the difference between right and wrong
singing out loud and dancing to my very own song
i face the mirror and stare at my reflection
these many years of life have dealt my direction

every lesson learned is merely a stepping stone
some follow and so many are spent alone
the path less traveled is the one i will take
for if not; it is my own soul i will forsake

it is love i give and all love i want to feel
from my heart; this i give of my own freewill
the fantasy filled expectations are not dreams
society clutters our minds with flawless schemes

the users and abusers try to take control
i thank the younger years; for this is my soul
walking thru all the memories of my life
i laugh and wonder why; i even cried

shards of glass

someone; can anyone please help me
on my knees praying for healthy
i have so much i want and need to say
wasted breath; not hearing me anyway

loving you; you never let me in
it was over before it ever did begin
held down with a heavy weight
for you; i do not want to hate

drowning in the tears i borrow
my unwanted soul feels so hollow
bleeding with so much pain
these emotions are driving me insane

from you; was it too much i did demand
a lonely, wilted rose i hold in my hand
broken heart that you cannot see
shards of glass inside of me

chamber of my dreams

i guess; i was way too blind to really see
had no idea that you wanted to be with me
the looks you would give across the way
wish; i could go back and change those days

glad to see that you are so very happy
feeling deep down inside that could be me
missing all those belly laughs we shared
wish; you had told me how much you cared

black and white and sometimes in color
you are there; makes no difference, whichever
long time ago you were within my reach
now you live in the chamber of my dreams

doors do open

the scent
of burned out candles

the smell of something old
the smell of something new

the
gate
waits

walk thru

power of your future
is found within you

time has passed

lost in nightly dreams of my painful past
between tears and silent screams i try to gasp
inside this body i search for inner peace
love i have for you i need and must release

emotions cascade thru every single memory
opening my swollen eyes; a desire for beauty
calling to my soul; no, please don't go
it's over and the long, drawn curtains are closed

what you offered; i deserve so much more
spreading my wings; high in the sky i will soar
disappearing thoughts of you; finally, at last
everything happens for a reason; time has passed

battle my cries

we were everything a loving couple should be
i pictured you spending this beautiful life with me
when i felt your touch; my heart would skip a beat
you were everything and all my soul ever did need

all of our perfect, future plans were set in stone
i cherished all of the precious moments spent alone
i believed every word you spoke from your lips
never imagined that we would ever end like this

that day in may; we made a vow to above
i never thought you would fall out of love
this is our final meeting and our last goodbye
leaving here all alone to battle my cries

for eternity

walking hand in hand on nature's dirt path
together we witness all the little critter's tracks
different timbers stretch to the blue sky
leaves dance in the beauty of your eyes

on the dock; we fish for blue gill, catfish and bass
oh how we wish our mini vacation would last
gorgeous color that matches the sun's glare
i love the way the breeze blows your hair

ripples in the water; remind me of your smile
going to sit here and stare at you for awhile
dragonflies chase and skim across the pond
i've fallen in love; in my heart you are the one

we both relax and just float in the rowboat
true love we share; neither of us gave up hope
admiring every moment of nature's marvelous beauty
here with you is where i want to be; for eternity

lonely avenue

all alone on this dark and lonely avenue
here i sit; heart broken, still waiting for you
my life; deep from my lungs i want to scream
crazy fears of alone enter my nightly dreams

on my own pouring tears; my throat chokes
feeling deep inside there is no more hope
mind occupied by years of sleepless nights
searching for the path; the one with the light

again; love melts thru my trembling hands
in search of the very soul that understands
here i sit; heart broken, still waiting for you
all alone; on this dark and lonely avenue

tattooed on my heart

you are the most beautiful song
for you; i have waited for so long
your blue eyes touch me physically
i am mesmerized by your words mentally

captivated by your positive energy
it is only you who completes me
hypnotized at the very sight of you
our hearts beat as one; no longer two

on my skin; such an amazing touch
do you know, i love you so very much
you are my daily, constant craving
with you; my life is a slice of heaven

for every single day that comes to pass
spending my time with you; a soul with class
my love; from me, you will never part
it is your name tattooed on my heart

a new love to explore

you make me smile; you make me laugh
you are becoming my sweet, better half
you are like a beautiful, red rose in bloom
within the walls of my heart; living in every room

every kiss we share takes me far away
wanting a love to last far past my dying day
your smile touches me so very deeply
amazing eyes; i adore the way you look at me

inside my soul; my emotions are reeling
sharing a life is such a wonderful feeling
moments we spend together; i cherish
without you; a part of me would perish

it is you that takes me on that romantic ride
we dance together; up high, on clouds in the sky
with you; i feel like a kid in a candy store
opening my heart; a new love to explore

lonely heart that led

once, you were the very flame in my darkness
realizing your lies how could you be so heartless
you haunt my memory with the games you played
settled and alone is where i should have stayed

i was special; your words planted the seed
years living with ugliness and pure greed
my heart suffers thru the days of your absence
my broken soul tarnished by your madness

settling for so much less than i deserved
believing you could change was absurd
my pouring tears; please get me past this pain
will never share my love again; i am not the same

gave you my heart for all the wrong reasons
alone again living thru the change of seasons
when thoughts of you enter my spinning head
i realize it was my lonely heart that led

words are not enough

on the phone; it's all about how much you miss me
when we are out you act as if we are only sisterly
you tell me i am the only one in your world
sure seems to me you were flirting with that girl

pouring your heart out; swearing, i am the one
when i ask you questions; you come undone
i complete all of your unanswered, future dreams
all your friends are far more important than me

you have never loved nor ever felt this way
i sure do; i see every single thing that you say
what i hear coming from your lips is just stuff
all your misrepresented words are not enough

beautiful, red rose

once; such a beautiful, red rose
needing so much water to grow
the abundant sunshine to flower
i am leaving you without power

your wicked thorns are very sharp
cutting so deep at this torn heart
your hurtful ways cause no strife
certainly not a part of my life

a promise today; i will part
tomorrow is born; a fresh start
you and i; we just don't click
now it's your turn to feel the prick

straight from the heart

the first time you caught my eye
my soul started to sing a lullaby
i always remembered your incredible smile
thinking; i want to stay with you a while

loved all those times we sat and talked all night
for me; being with you just felt so right
that night we watched a movie and held hands
my feelings for you would never be the same again

the evening we shared our first slow dance
my wondering mind; would i have a chance
i will never forget that first kiss i gave you
shocked myself; that was right out of the blue

day we walked on the beach, listening to the sea
wanting you for the rest of my life; just you and me
you are the one i've needed right from the start
these words are true; straight from the heart

i remember

i remember when we wrote our initials in the sand

i remember that beautiful day i held your hand

i remember the way i got lost in your eyes

i remember that field where we ran off to hide

i remember how we shared our very first kiss

i remember thinking i always want to feel this

i remember how we just fit like a glove

i remember the very moment i fell in love

i remember the day you admitted to your lies

i remember falling to my knees praying to the sky

i remember when i finally forgot your name

and

i remember at that very second my life changed

kiss me in the rain

never thought i could ever feel this way
your amazing touch washed away all of my pain
enjoying this love we share every, single day
with you; all of me is here to stay

you live deep down inside my beating heart
such an amazing soul; a marvelous piece of art
i sleep at night and ever so peacefully
feeling your true love right here with me

waking to the sound of an incredible thunderstorm
here inside me; the one and only i so adore
calling to you by your beautiful name
come walk with me and kiss me in the rain

fly my broken soul home

living in a fairy tale land built on perfection
mirror clouded; struggling with self reflection
in a state of denial; bound by these rusty chains
reliving mistakes of love; caught in so much pain

wondering what actually brought me to this place
the deepest scars on my face i need to escape
drowning in sorrow; distraught heart in despair
deserted feelings; lonely, left without a care

searching for courage and strength to just let go
lost in a whirlwind of emotion; unstable, i grow
the return to innocence is all i need to find
past the stars i stare; my only vision of divine

pretending to be happy seems to help me cope
darkness falls; crying myself to sleep, losing hope
this journey called life is so empty; me, i'm all alone
wish i had the wings to fly my broken soul home

how sweet it is

stunning blue eyes; captivating every ounce of my being
everything i see in you; it is my heart you are stealing
a touch that drives goose bumps across my trembling body
i have never felt this way; never, not with anybody

a mesmerizing scent of you enters every single room
amazing fragrance of a garden of red roses in bloom
voice that is as soft as flowing music to my ears
i want to hear your beautiful melody for years

an amazing smile that brightens my dark evening sky
with you; under the summer stars i want to lie
all night long; i feel you there, dancing in my dreams
knowing you are the only one for me; i sleep peacefully

i melt at the very sight of your forever, loving soul
in love with wonderful you; i just have to let you know
with you; i enjoy every single moment of our bliss
my lips can't get enough of your kiss; how sweet it is

forever in love

all of our time we spend together
each day just gets better and better
when your soft hands touch my skin
you take me to a place i've never been

and every single time our lips kiss
i experience a feeling of wonderful bliss
you are all i want and ever need
only you complete all of my dreams

a wonderful soul swept me off my feet
you definitely have my heart for keeps
is this forever always your enough
the two of us; forever in love

your constant scars

why doesn't my family have faith in me?
make changes within you; they will believe
a broken heart and i can't bare to let go?
if you don't leave town there is no next show

i need a lover; why am i so very lonely?
true happiness is found within you honey
why does bad always come my way?
it's time to close those open doors; today

someone tell me, when will i ever be happy?
when you stop looking for love; it's so sappy
i want to be complete; who is going to love me?
it is much more complicated; look very deep

i want a better life; what should i do?
bottom line; all you have, is the trust of you
to move on; no matter how near or far
you cannot live with your constant scars

my surprise

you; definitely my surprise

start of a million shared highs

just us; safe, no more cries

lullabies, songs and butterflies

wee hours our shared dreams fly

next to me your lovely heart lies

we dance together at midnight

our amazing love is in flight

us; far apart with closed eyes

certainly not our goodbyes

merely the start of our lives

you; definitely my surprise

thief of emotions

i reach for you and you are no longer there
unfulfilled love; you and not one single care
these lost moments of my life i try to find
you are the only part i wish i could rewind

searching for the release of this heartbreak
you definitely prove to be my biggest mistake
within me; a fight i am losing to a broken soul
night after night; it is you i so try to let go

my mind out of focus and a path so unclear
here alone; trying to live without you dear
my tears cannot wash away this horrible pain
struggling every second trying to reach my sane

seems each day shortens and my sadness grows
to experience a true love; it is all i want to know
over and over; you take hearts as your tokens
you are nothing more than a thief of emotions

a perfect melody

every single night in my journal i write
my thoughts of you in constant flight
like a butterfly that soars thru the sky
for so long i've waited for just you and i

every time i see you my heart flutters
whispers in my mind; i love you, i utter
building a foundation one brick at a time
forever in my heart you will be mine

springtime; new life, beautiful flowers bloom
this heart of mine; no one else, no more room
everyday of our lives i want you beside me
our gorgeous song we sing; a perfect melody

slaughtered by your lies

all i wanted was you to be in my life
my expectations have turned to sacrifice
love to share; needing someone who cares
our sweet dreams have turned to nightmares

so many nights i lie awake; i need sleep
your harsh, hurtful words cut me so deep
praying for strength; please, give me able
excessive temper tantrums; you are unstable

ego in defeat; leaving you with all your scars
i lost my soul somewhere deep within the stars
it is time for me to part; hear my goodbyes
a broken heart; slaughtered by your lies

taken by the best

your contagious smile brightens all of my days
the way you make me laugh; i'm just amazed
you possess such a warm and tender touch
no words can express how i enjoy you so much

and those hypnotizing, deep, blue eyes
lost in all of you; captivated and mesmerized
you take my very breath away with your kiss
without you; a huge part of my soul i miss

brilliant mind; keeps me on my toes all the time
makes me so happy to know you are all mine
this is where my heart will forever live and rest
here with you; i have been, taken by the best

never, ever comes

nightly; you wish upon a star for true love
the twinkle fades and it never, ever comes
trying to hold back tears you want to cry
urge to live in the reflection of special eyes

a beautiful love you so want to share
just searching for someone who will care
breaths of fresh air keep you alive
without it; your broken, torn heart will die

the emotion a lonely soul does so miss
it is the caress of another's tenderness
sitting alone on a dark, moonlit night
seems your one dream is out of sight

praying someone will hold your heart for keeps
you drift to sleep and enter abandoned dreams
nightly; you wish upon a star for true love
the twinkle fades and it never, ever comes

living our love song

a beautiful melody sung from our hearts
two souls born to be and will never part
intoxicated by the warmth in your smile
you are the feeling i haven't felt in a while

very blessed for each day spent together
not one storm you and i cannot weather
magic in your touch; my butterflies dance
with you lover; sharing a lifelong romance

your wonderful voice is music to my ears
for someone so dear; i have waited years
a vow to cause no harm or do no wrong
you and i; we are living our love song

sadness of a soul

love to some; simply seems like a game
caught; they show not an ounce of shame
there is so much of me i want to share
somewhere is someone who truly cares

looking for a simple way to free myself
searching stars above; in dire need of help
without you in my life; daily, i try to cope
waking to sunshine; just praying for hope

all your lies bounce around in my memory
this is the way you are; finally, i can see
it is my pain; learning to finally let go
tears fall to cleanse the sadness of a soul

to be saved

born from the same parents
why does hatred even exist
in a hand basket society rides
it will not work; a love disguise

food and drug administration
each pill; a personal poison
priding on a country of christian
venom seeps from our system

breaking all the rules along the way
on your knees you pray; to be saved
so many lies floating around
super power to a country clown

full of hate and full of doubt
time to stand up and shout out loud
who in the hell has your soul
respect or control; which do you hold

whisper from your lips

invincible and so smooth; you enter my nightly dreams
   gliding in as if you are an angel but bare black wings
the endless dark hours we spend in our solidarity scene
   taking me away to a mystical place; i can barely breathe

   mind struggles with silent screams; my voice is mute
   pack of wolves howl and in the distance an owl hoots
     dressed in red and holding torches; your choir sings
   organ pipes play a death song melody; church bells ring

exhausted; you leave with a shadow that follows moonlight
   i lie in blood, gasping for air; alone, left here just to die
thru walls of my beating heart and to the bottom they rip
   are the words of poison you whisper from your lips